The Longman Anthology
of British Literature

VOLUME 2C

THE TWENTIETH CENTURY

David Damrosch
COLUMBIA UNIVERSITY

Christopher Baswell
UNIVERSITY OF CALIFORNIA, LOS ANGELES

Clare Carroll
QUEENS COLLEGE, CITY UNIVERSITY OF NEW YORK

Kevin J. H. Dettmar
SOUTHERN ILLINOIS UNIVERSITY

Heather Henderson

Constance Jordan
CLAREMONT GRADUATE UNIVERSITY

Peter J. Manning
STATE UNIVERSITY OF NEW YORK, STONY BROOK

Anne Howland Schotter
WAGNER COLLEGE

William Chapman Sharpe
BARNARD COLLEGE

Stuart Sherman
FORDHAM UNIVERSITY

Jennifer Wicke
UNIVERSITY OF VIRGINIA

Susan J. Wolfson
PRINCETON UNIVERSITY

The Longman Anthology of British Literature

Second Edition

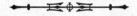

David Damrosch

General Editor

VOLUME 2C

THE TWENTIETH CENTURY
Kevin Dettmar *and* Jennifer Wicke

Longman

New York   San Francisco   Boston
London   Toronto   Sydney   Tokyo   Singapore   Madrid
Mexico City   Munich   Paris   Cape Town   Hong Kong   Montreal

CONTENTS

⇒✦ PERSPECTIVES ✦⇐
The Great War: Confronting the Modern   2167

SPEECHES ON IRISH INDEPENDENCE   2232

WILLIAM BUTLER YEATS   2242